Make A
Joyful Noise!!!

Ry Zt

Congratulations!

Please insert either the CD or the DVD attached inside the front cover to begin enjoying the most comprehensive entertainment experience available for *The Velveteen Rabbit: An Illustrated Rock Opera*

Hear it again like you've never heard it before.

This multimedia project provides:

- a Symphonic Rock n' Roll Soundtrack on CD,
- a Cinema|Audio Experience on DVD, and
- a fully Illustrated Lyric Book

Our project, like the classic Margery Williams story, touches the hearts of generations of countless families filled with children growing and with children grown.

For a hi-fidelity audio experience, please insert the Symphonic Rock n' Roll Soundtrack CD into your favorite player and follow along in the richly colored Illustrated Lyric Book. Or, if you wish to enjoy a visual feast of sound and sight in vivid color on a viewing screen of your choice, please insert the Cinema|Audio Experience on DVD into your favorite player while you follow the lyrics in the Illustrated Lyric Book.

But, regardless of which enjoyment experience you choose, we want to thank you for sharing your time with us. By viewing and hearing this project you'll be treated to over an hour's worth of songs, music, and narration that will reveal to you and your family the truth that Bunny finally learns. The truth of knowing that "Life's A Gift."

Literatunes

presents

the Velveteen Rabbit
An Illustrated Rock Opera

Musical Compositions and Libretto
by
Ryan Nelson Stevens

Illustrations
by
Candice Purwin

Requests for permission to make copies of any part of the work should
be mailed to the following address:
Permission Department,
Opti-Mystic LLC d/b/a Literatunes,
201 Azalea Key Lane, Chapin SC 29036

Library of Congress Control Number: 2009902948

ISBN 10   0-9823872-3-7 combined print book, CD audio book,
DVD audio/visual book
ISBN 13   978-0-9823872-3-8 combined print book, CD audio book,
DVD audio/visual book

Printed in China by asianprinting.com

Book Design by Taylor Barnes of L7 Studio
Venice, California

Vocal Performances on CD and DVD:
Wendi Freeman as "Bunny"
Ryan Nelson Stevens – remainder

CONTENTS

ACT ONE

ACT TWO

CAST OF CHARACTERS

Bunny, The Velveteen Rabbit
The Boy
Skins, An Old & Weathered Toy Horse
Nana, The Boy's Guardian
Doctor, MD
The Mechanical Robots
Timothy, The Wooden Lion
HMS, The Model Sailboat
Gibb Gray, The Real Rabbit
&
Art, The Narrator

Life's A Gift...

La-la-la-la-la-la-la-la-la La-la-la-la-la-la-la-la-la-la Life's a gift

La-la-la-la-la-la-la-la-la-la Life's a gift

What will you make of it?

What will you take from it?

La-la-la-la-la-la-la-la-la-la-la-la-la Life's a gift

La-la-la-la-la-la-la-la-la-la-la Life's a gift

And yet we're always wanting more

What will you do with yours?

What will you do with yours?

What will you do with yours?

What will you do with yours?

What will you do with yours?

What will you do with yours?

TAILS

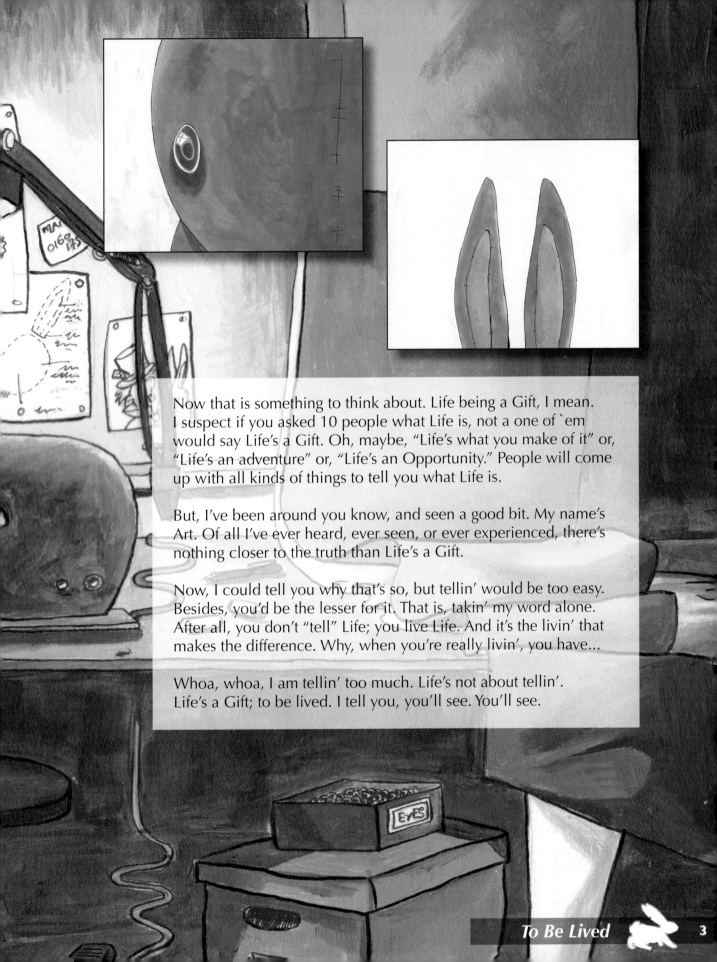

Now that is something to think about. Life being a Gift, I mean.
I suspect if you asked 10 people what Life is, not a one of `em
would say Life's a Gift. Oh, maybe, "Life's what you make of it" or,
"Life's an adventure" or, "Life's an Opportunity." People will come
up with all kinds of things to tell you what Life is.

But, I've been around you know, and seen a good bit. My name's
Art. Of all I've ever heard, ever seen, or ever experienced, there's
nothing closer to the truth than Life's a Gift.

Now, I could tell you why that's so, but tellin' would be too easy.
Besides, you'd be the lesser for it. That is, takin' my word alone.
After all, you don't "tell" Life; you live Life. And it's the livin' that
makes the difference. Why, when you're really livin', you have...

Whoa, whoa, I am tellin' too much. Life's not about tellin'.
Life's a Gift; to be lived. I tell you, you'll see. You'll see.

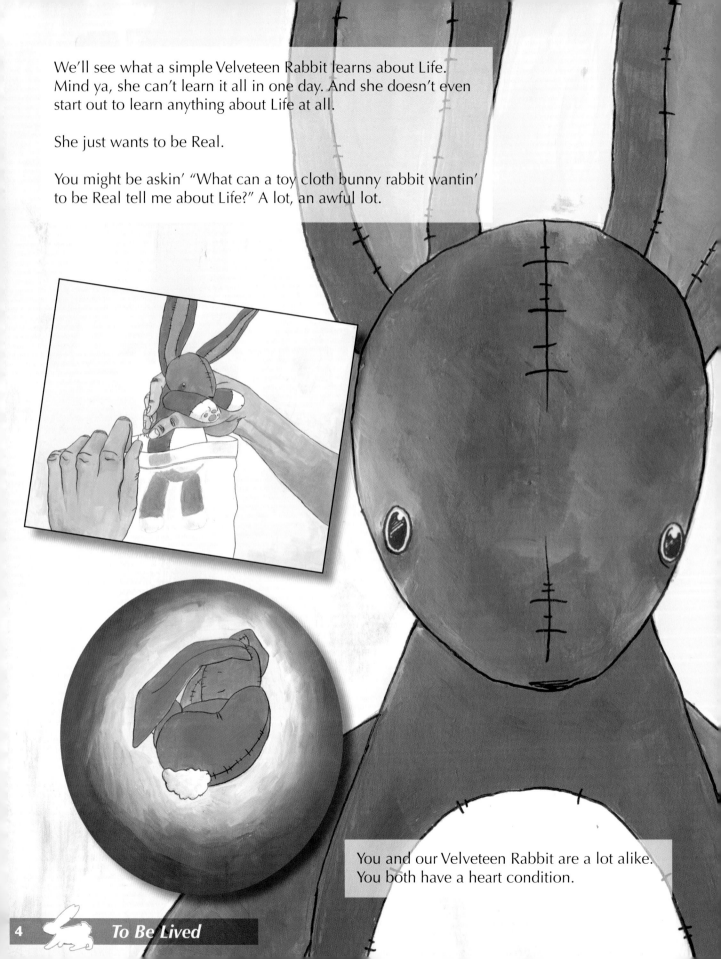

We'll see what a simple Velveteen Rabbit learns about Life.
Mind ya, she can't learn it all in one day. And she doesn't even
start out to learn anything about Life at all.

She just wants to be Real.

You might be askin' "What can a toy cloth bunny rabbit wantin'
to be Real tell me about Life?" A lot, an awful lot.

You and our Velveteen Rabbit are a lot alike.
You both have a heart condition.

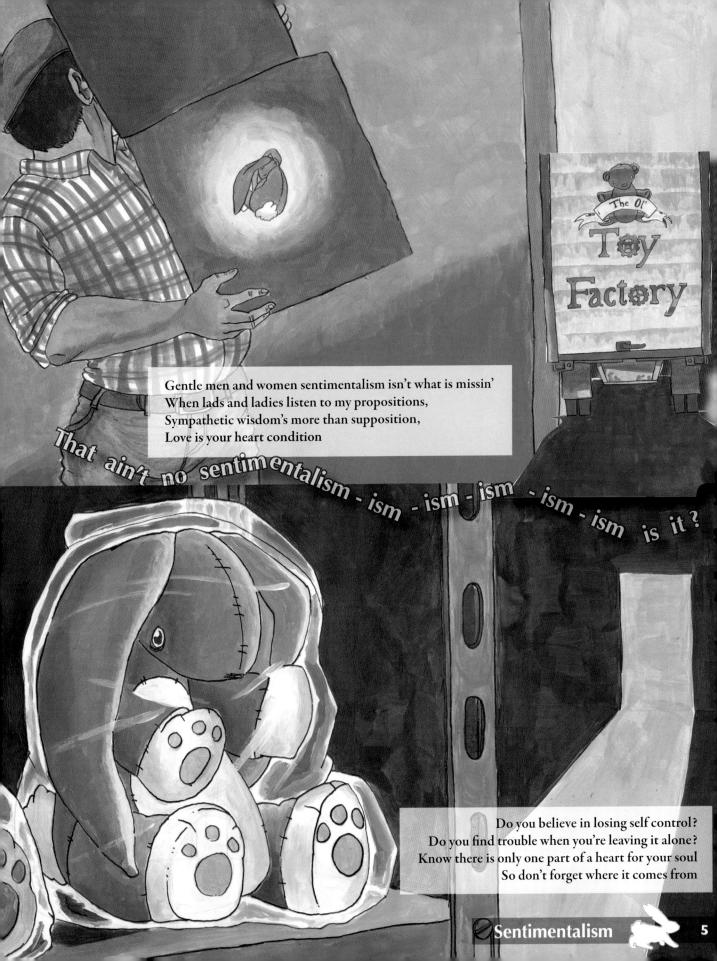

Gentle men and women sentimentalism isn't what is missin'
When lads and ladies listen to my propositions,
Sympathetic wisdom's more than supposition,
Love is your heart condition

That ain't no sentimentalism - ism - ism - ism - ism - ism - ism is it?

Do you believe in losing self control?
Do you find trouble when you're leaving it alone?
Know there is only one part of a heart for your soul
So don't forget where it comes from

Sentimentalism

If you ponder why some loves die in the heart long before the mind

Well you might resign your self, go and find Divine design

A life spent loving refines, refines, refines, refines, refines

Friend, are you that kind?

A heart condition. Love: it is a heart condition.
Friends, you've got to find that out first.
So, whether your heart is Velveteen or Pre-teen,
you can't learn much about Life being a Gift until
you ask that first really big question. "Does love live here?"
If someone searched your heart, what would they find?
Well, that's one you've got to answer for yourself.

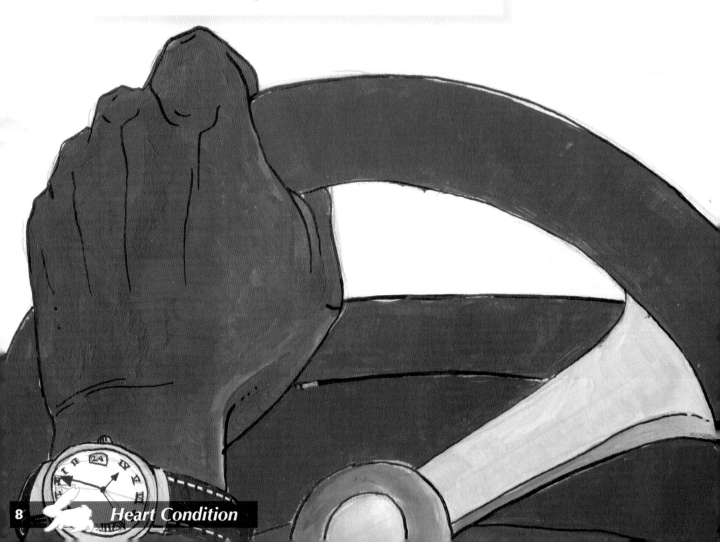

But to answer that question
for our rabbit friend,
our story takes us to
Christmas morning.
Our Bunny is a shiny and
plumb Velveteen Rabbit,
and she makes a
right handsome appearance sittin'
in that Christmas stockin'.

Very soon, very soon,
an excited 6 year old boy
will start the process that I've seen
over and over again,
countless times before.
Oh, no, not just with toy rabbits
and little boys,
but with people the world over.
All ages, all types, all the same.
Each has an opportunity
so magnificent, so unbelievable,
that words are just inadequate.
But then, like I said,
Life's not for tellin',
it's for livin'.

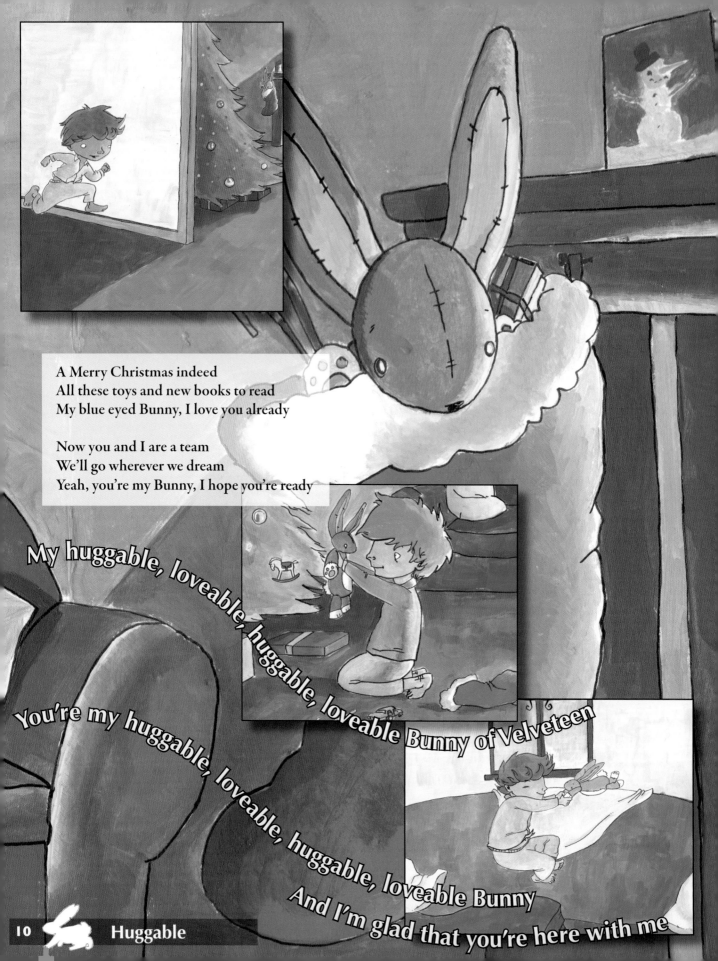

A Merry Christmas indeed
All these toys and new books to read
My blue eyed Bunny, I love you already

Now you and I are a team
We'll go wherever we dream
Yeah, you're my Bunny, I hope you're ready

My huggable, loveable, huggable, loveable Bunny of Velveteen

You're my huggable, loveable, huggable, loveable Bunny
And I'm glad that you're here with me

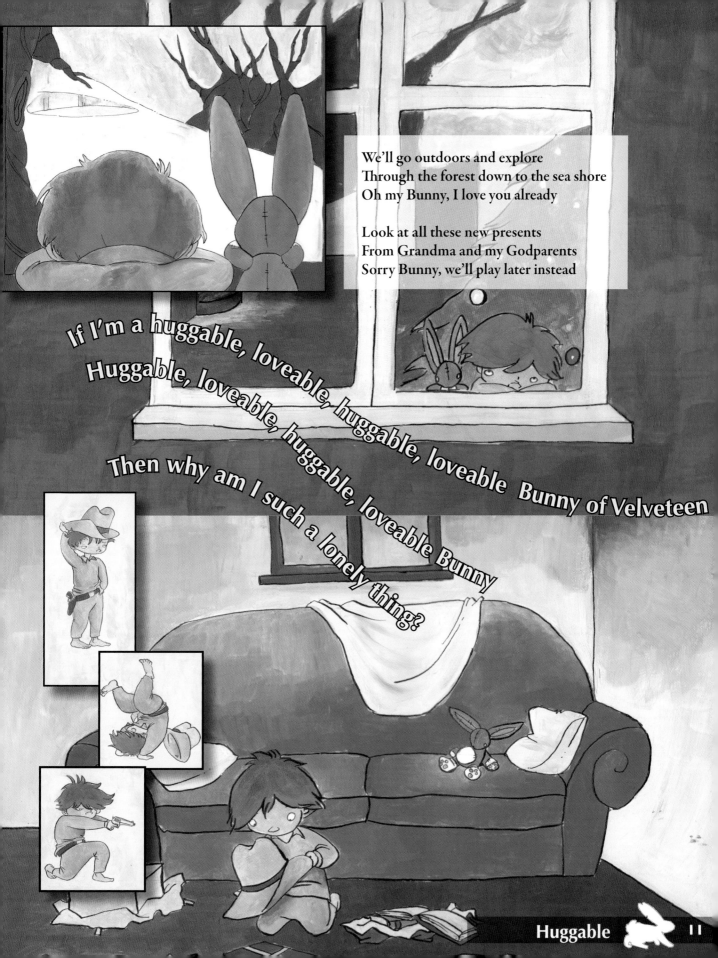

We'll go outdoors and explore
Through the forest down to the sea shore
Oh my Bunny, I love you already

Look at all these new presents
From Grandma and my Godparents
Sorry Bunny, we'll play later instead

If I'm a huggable, loveable,
Huggable, loveable, huggable, loveable Bunny of Velveteen
Then why am I such a lonely thing?

My huggable, loveable, huggable, loveable Bunny of Velveteen
Huggable, loveable, huggable, loveable Bunny
Then why am I such a lonely thing?

Why, why, why? Why am I so lonely?
Why, why, why? Why did the Boy disown me?

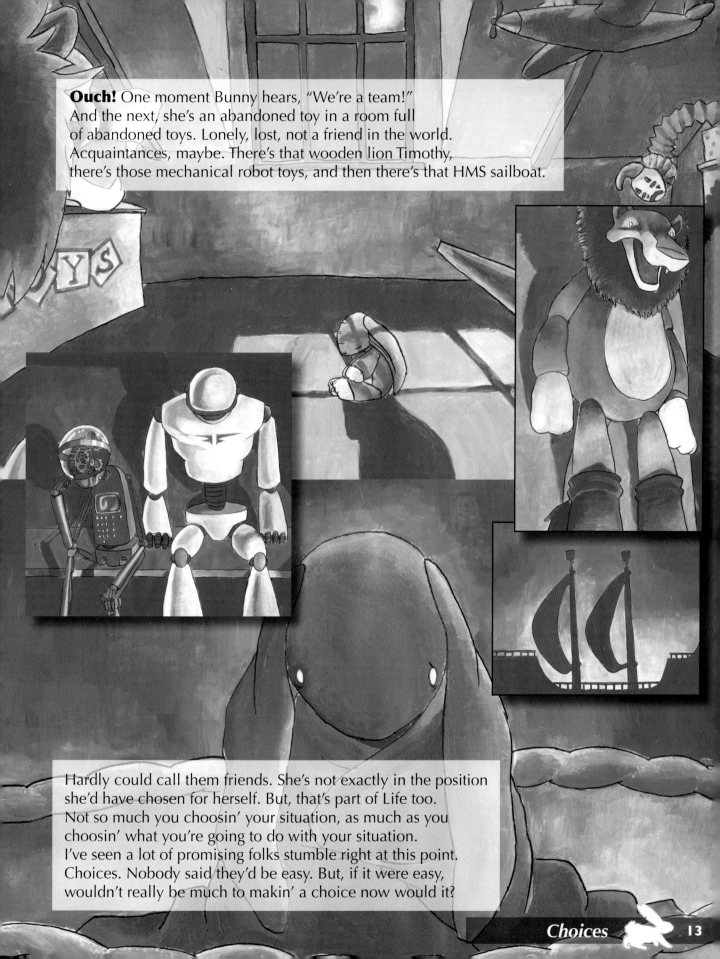

Ouch! One moment Bunny hears, "We're a team!"
And the next, she's an abandoned toy in a room full
of abandoned toys. Lonely, lost, not a friend in the world.
Acquaintances, maybe. There's that wooden lion Timothy,
there's those mechanical robot toys, and then there's that HMS sailboat.

Hardly could call them friends. She's not exactly in the position
she'd have chosen for herself. But, that's part of Life too.
Not so much you choosin' your situation, as much as you
choosin' what you're going to do with your situation.
I've seen a lot of promising folks stumble right at this point.
Choices. Nobody said they'd be easy. But, if it were easy,
wouldn't really be much to makin' a choice now would it?

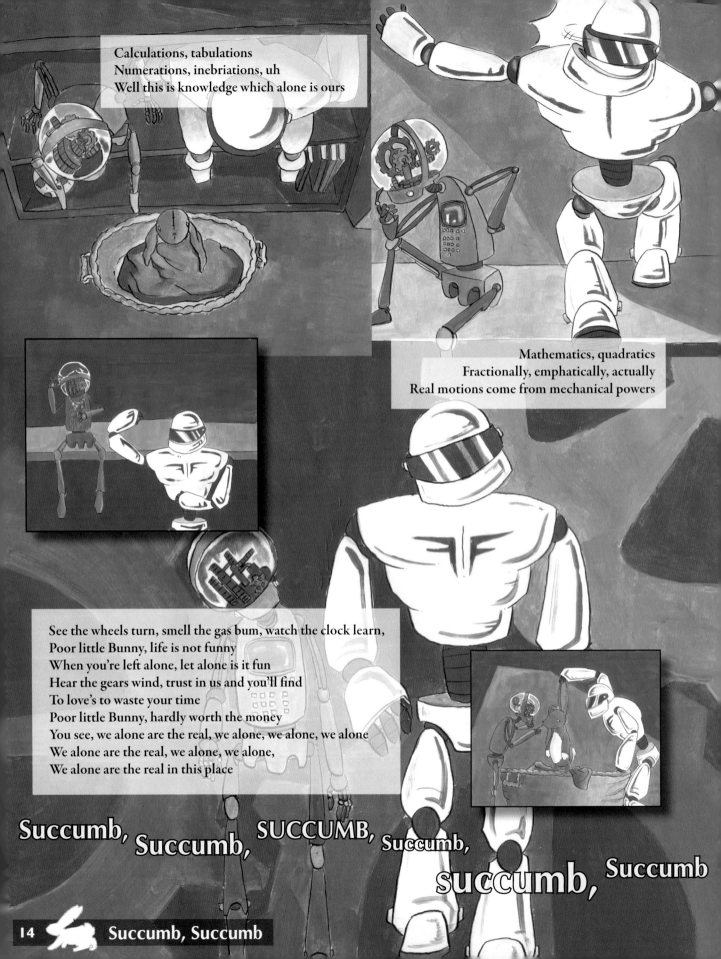

Calculations, tabulations
Numerations, inebriations, uh
Well this is knowledge which alone is ours

Mathematics, quadratics
Fractionally, emphatically, actually
Real motions come from mechanical powers

See the wheels turn, smell the gas bum, watch the clock learn,
Poor little Bunny, life is not funny
When you're left alone, let alone is it fun
Hear the gears wind, trust in us and you'll find
To love's to waste your time
Poor little Bunny, hardly worth the money
You see, we alone are the real, we alone, we alone, we alone
We alone are the real, we alone, we alone,
We alone are the real in this place

Succumb, Succumb, SUCCUMB, Succumb, succumb, Succumb

Well spare me these trivialities
I'd sooner give more cares for fleas
But as I'm crafted of finest wood
I say the worrying would do me no good
So step aside, the King of the Nursery am I
Call me Lord Timothy and that will suffice,
yeah that will suffice

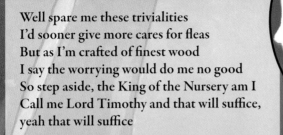

You see your young Bunny-ness
There are finer, broader views to address
You'd do well to listen to my guidance
You'd have my ear for your every confiding
Just walk with Lord Timothy, King of the Nursery
You and I shall slight the time observing reality

See the wheels turn, smell the gas bum, watch the clock learn,
You poor little Bunny, life smites you honey
And more than once or twice, you'll need someone's advice
Hear my joints' creak, trust in me when I speak
To love's to love to be weak
Poor little Bunny, you're hardly worth the money
You see, we alone are the real, we alone, we alone, we alone
We alone are the real, we alone,
We alone are the real in this place

Succumb, Succumb, SUCCUMB, Succumb,

succumb, Succumb

Oh well my lady Bunny if you might permit me
My contemptuous mates now seek again to forget me
Was it not I that sailed the gales of the mighty Atlantic
When clueless Columbus became so seasick and frantic?

Well the mainmast splintered and we approached shipwreck
But I scurried the sailors to safety below the deck
I leveled the horizon and I steadied my bow
While those cowards just kept repeating their vows

Fury from the starboard, hail from the port
I bullied the ocean with my bulk-headed retort
And now I know I'm the purest model of Her Majesty's Sailboat
For my every scratch is proud to prove, ooh, this vessel can float

Succumb, Succumb

See my bold stem, feel the jib turn, watch the stars learn,
Poor little Bunny, life is not funny
When you're left alone, let alone is it fun
Taste the salty air, glory is out there
But love's too much to bear
You poor little Bunny, you're hardly worth the money
You see, we alone are the real, we alone, we alone, we alone
We alone are the real, we alone, we alone,
We alone are the real in this place

We alone are the real in this place...

Succumb, Succumb, SUCCUMB, Succumb, succumb, Succumb

We alone are the real in this place little Bunny,
You should remember that

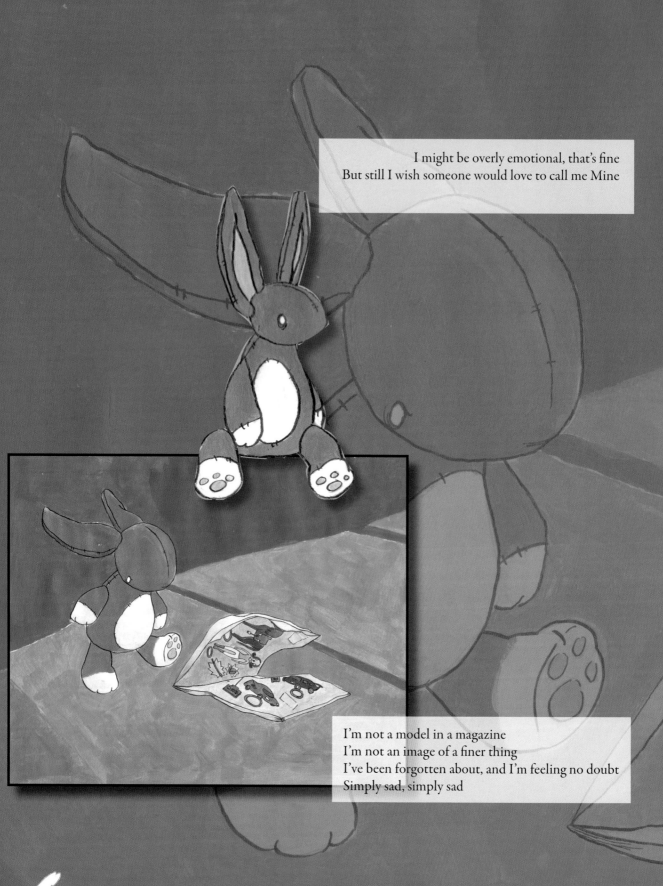

I might be overly emotional, that's fine
But still I wish someone would love to call me Mine

I'm not a model in a magazine
I'm not an image of a finer thing
I've been forgotten about, and I'm feeling no doubt
Simply sad, simply sad

Because I can't change what's arranged
In this life in store for me, and I need a friend
I'd cry to burst to see why it hurts
Was I made in vain, please explain, oh I need a friend
Oh please explain, oh I need a friend

I say, hey, there's never the perfect occasion for
Melancholy tears, not with so much to be thankful for
No you won't find me in the magazines
But you know I know that I'm something
Plus, them toys ain't real, they're just jealous wood and steel
They're simply mad, hmm-hmm-hmm, simply mad

You see, I can't change what's arranged
In this life in store for me and I need a friend
Skins is my name, I'm retired from fame
But whether you're fancy or plain we're all the same,
Yep, we all need a friend
We're all the same, yep, we all need a friend

Skins, what is real? Is it something you can feel?
Is it made of fancy parts? I've only got a sawdust heart
And that's no technological innovation
I'm afraid I don't have the right qualifications

It ain't your looks or how you're made
It's a miracle you become one day
It takes the true love and touch of a child
It nearly breaks you, but it's worth your while
`Cause when you're real you feel a different way
And that's all there is to say about
That's all there is to say about
That's all there is to say about that

No I can't change what's arranged
In this life in store for me, but I need a friend
Find someone to hold you nights through
Days and days and back and forth again
Find someone to hold you nights through
Days and days and back and forth again

`Cause we're all the same, yep, we all need a friend
Yeah, we are the same, yep, we all need a friend
`Cause we are the same, yep, we all need a friend
We all need a friend, we all need a friend

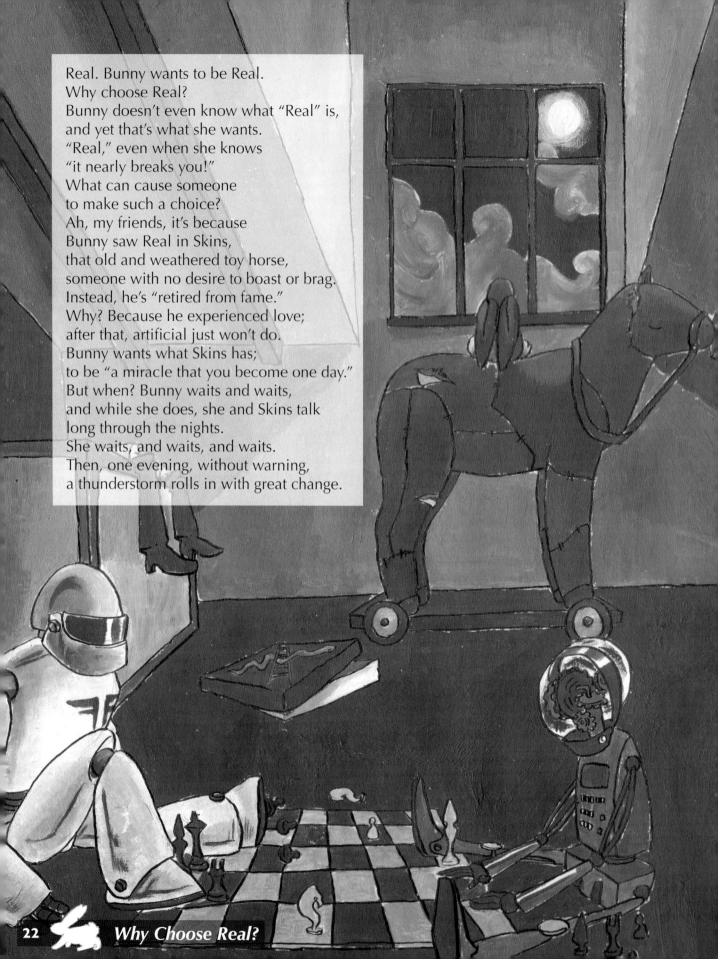

Real. Bunny wants to be Real.
Why choose Real?
Bunny doesn't even know what "Real" is,
and yet that's what she wants.
"Real," even when she knows
"it nearly breaks you!"
What can cause someone
to make such a choice?
Ah, my friends, it's because
Bunny saw Real in Skins,
that old and weathered toy horse,
someone with no desire to boast or brag.
Instead, he's "retired from fame."
Why? Because he experienced love;
after that, artificial just won't do.
Bunny wants what Skins has;
to be "a miracle that you become one day."
But when? Bunny waits and waits,
and while she does, she and Skins talk
long through the nights.
She waits, and waits, and waits.
Then, one evening, without warning,
a thunderstorm rolls in with great change.

Here comes the thunder rolling
With no flash of lightning for warning
We fear the whirlwinds' tolling
Sweeping us to our cupboards `til morning
Sweeping us to our cupboards `til morning

These miniature monsters and crooks
A silly soldier with a helmet on his head,
making me see red
This cluster of dusty and musty old books
Which I know for sure the Boy has never read,
at least not yet
These piles and piles, piles and piles of more stuff
But now's the time for tidying up
Oh yes, now's the time for tidying up

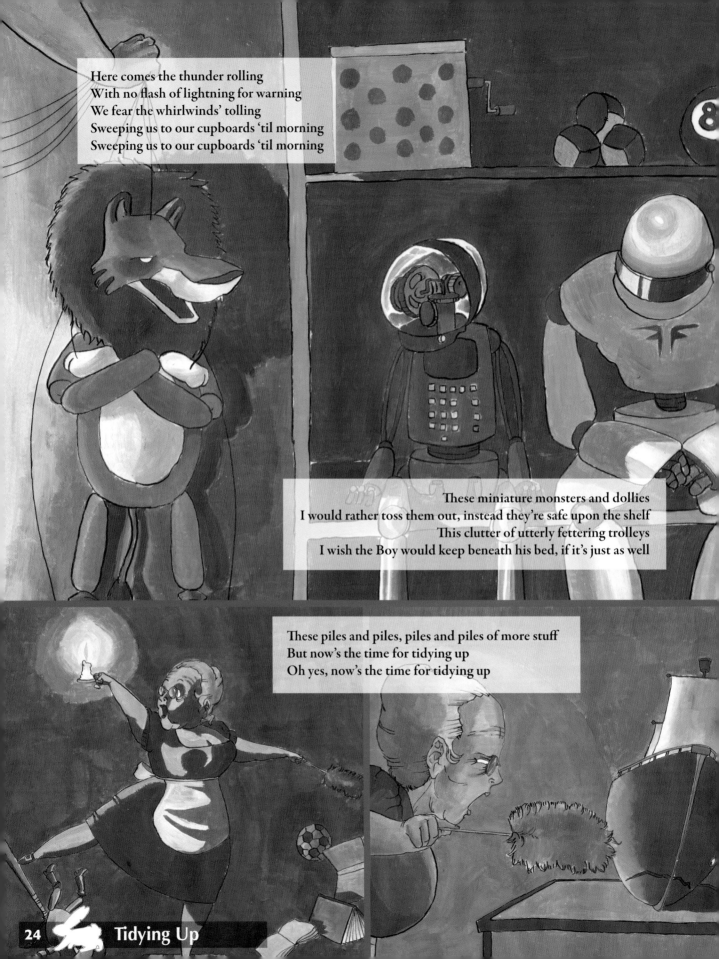

Here comes the thunder rolling
With no flash of lightning for warning
We fear the whirlwinds' tolling
Sweeping us to our cupboards 'til morning
Sweeping us to our cupboards 'til morning

These miniature monsters and dollies
I would rather toss them out, instead they're safe upon the shelf
This clutter of utterly fettering trolleys
I wish the Boy would keep beneath his bed, if it's just as well

These piles and piles, piles and piles of more stuff
But now's the time for tidying up
Oh yes, now's the time for tidying up

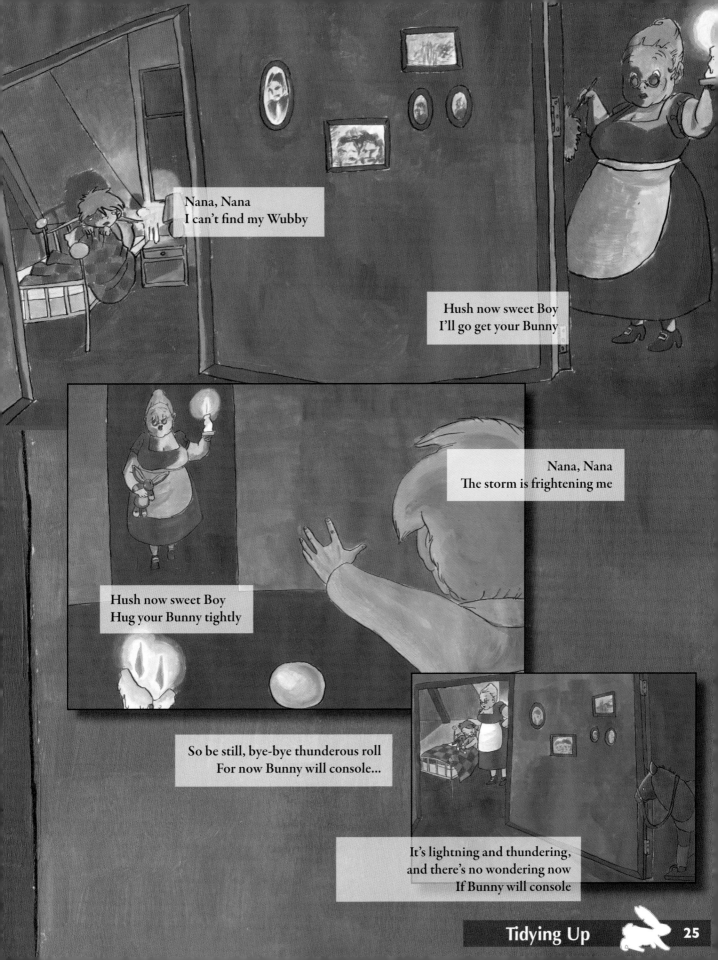

The storm outside crashes across the toy nursery, rumbling through the boy's room. It interrupts the world of Skins and Bunny. In a moment Bunny is taken. In an instant, Skins must remain behind.

At first, Bunny misses her long talks with Skins.
But she soon finds the Boy is kind, he's thoughtful,
he's creative; he's a ball of energy. He's all boy.
Bunny warms quickly to her new friend
and the two are inseparable.
He loves her and she loves him.
She wonders if this is what Skins meant?
Is this what it means to become "Real"?

I'm just lying here peacefully
Trying to catch a bit of quality sleep
And when my rest, feels at its best
Boy snuggles up tight as a peep

His breath is hot
Though I cannot pull away
And the bed becomes unbearable shoved beneath his pillow
I wish that I knew
What Skins would do in my place
Then the Boy talks with me about a world beyond his window
And wouldn't you know, I'm sold on love

Time escapes with all my sadness before my very eyes
Days, weeks and seasons, the more the merrier pass us by
With hardly a pause to notice any weathering of my fur
Boy never stops the fun to wonder what's wrong with her

In the summer haze we link a bond between child and pet
Fond feelings are immortalized in the bliss of red sunset
With scarce a chance to remember those haughty toys
Blinded by a change of heart I have for this dear boy
And wouldn't you know, I'm sold on love

Hey Bunny check out these tunnels I'm building for you
He helps me burrow down like he says the other rabbits do
Hey Bunny let's play the game where you guess what I'm thinking of
If I can't figure it out he laughs and says, close enough

Hey Bunny this wagon's your car and I'll be your driver
We're tearing `cross the lawn until we pop a tire
Hey Bunny this is your home where you and I can play
I'm left behind when he's suddenly called away

And I'm just lying here anxiously
In the flowers beneath a tree
I'm all alone, but then I see
Nana come looking for me

He pleads for his friend
It's hard for me to comprehend
But the bed becomes unbearable alone with just your pillow
I'll go grab it
So he'll have his favorite rabbit
The Boy deserves a better world behind his bedroom window

I hope his sleep is made complete
With his old Bunny at his cheek
Sorry if you find me more than a tad annoyed
Why all this fuss over a silly little toy?

Please give me my Bunny
You don't understand
She's real, she can hear you, she can

I can't believe what I just heard
He finally said the magic word
If Skins were here he'd smile at you know who
I guess everything he said is true

I am a miracle
I am hysterical
`Cause love's gotta hold on my heart
It never tatters
It's all that matters
`Cause love's gotta hold on my heart,
So please, please hold on heart
Please, please hold on heart

Dear Boy see your toy
She seems so much more
There's a look of real which wasn't there before

Hold On Heart

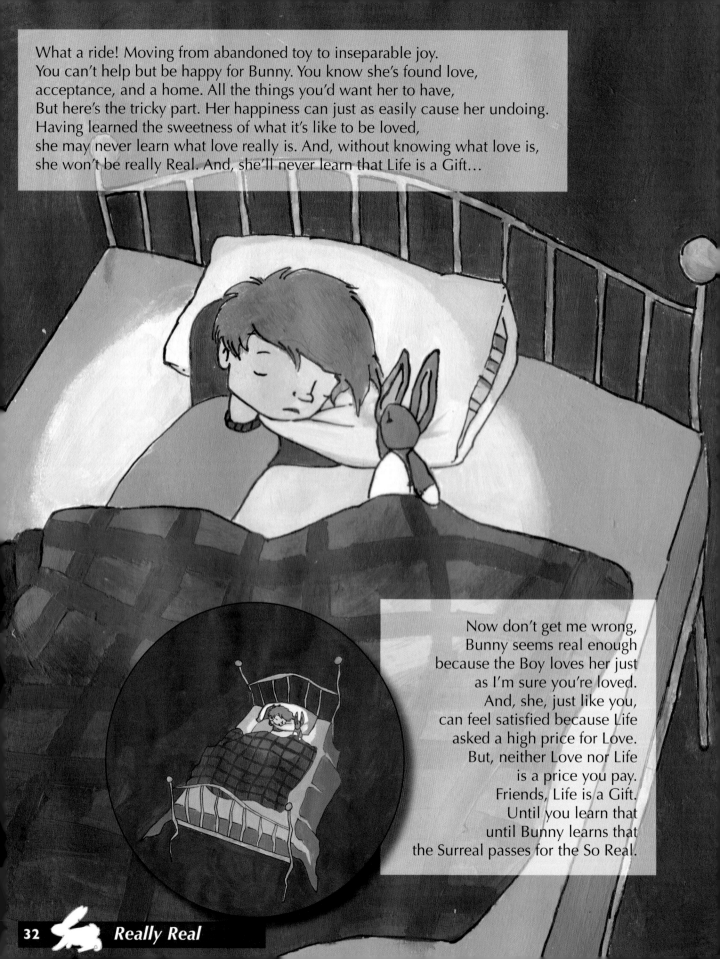

What a ride! Moving from abandoned toy to inseparable joy.
You can't help but be happy for Bunny. You know she's found love,
acceptance, and a home. All the things you'd want her to have,
But here's the tricky part. Her happiness can just as easily cause her undoing.
Having learned the sweetness of what it's like to be loved,
she may never learn what love really is. And, without knowing what love is,
she won't be really Real. And, she'll never learn that Life is a Gift…

Now don't get me wrong,
Bunny seems real enough
because the Boy loves her just
as I'm sure you're loved.
And, she, just like you,
can feel satisfied because Life
asked a high price for Love.
But, neither Love nor Life
is a price you pay.
Friends, Life is a Gift.
Until you learn that
until Bunny learns that
the Surreal passes for the So Real.

Life is a gift
you're realizing if

You come to know
you must reap what you sow

Life as it is,
a bliss no more than this

Sound in your heart,
keeps in tune with the part

Free your love from all of your fret
Learn to forgive and you can forget

Those classical cravings
for connectible ravings

If you try a little less and love,
then you will be you

The pattern that's playing
suggests a sensible saying

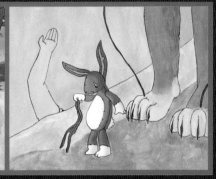

Like innocence is in a sense
not beyond you

Then you'll know the truth
of what I must mean

When you learn it's tough
to choose between

The surreal or so real,
Surreal or so real,

Surreal Or So Real?

Surreal or so real,
the surreal or so, so real

But is to touch as to feel?

Life is a gift,
you give it as you get

No failure for hope
`cause grace will help you cope

Life is all of this,
today tomorrow lets

You off your lonely shelf
you may recreate yourself

Free love is not just for some
For all lives have real freedom from

Those classical cravings
for connectible ravings

If you try a little less and love,
then you will be you

The pattern that's playing
suggests a sensible saying

Like innocence is in a sense
not beyond you

Then you'll know the truth
of what I must mean

When you learn it's tough
to choose between

The surreal or so real,
Surreal or so real,
Surreal or so real,
the surreal or so, so real

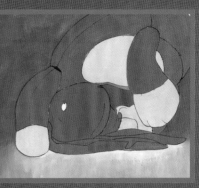

But is to touch as to
fee-e-e-e-e-e-e-e-e-e-e-eel?

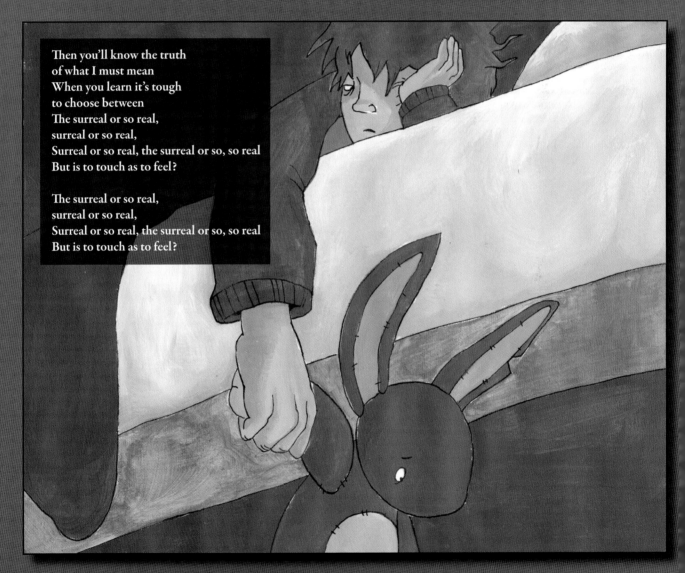

Then you'll know the truth
of what I must mean
When you learn it's tough
to choose between
The surreal or so real,
surreal or so real,
Surreal or so real, the surreal or so, so real
But is to touch as to feel?

The surreal or so real,
surreal or so real,
Surreal or so real, the surreal or so, so real
But is to touch as to feel?

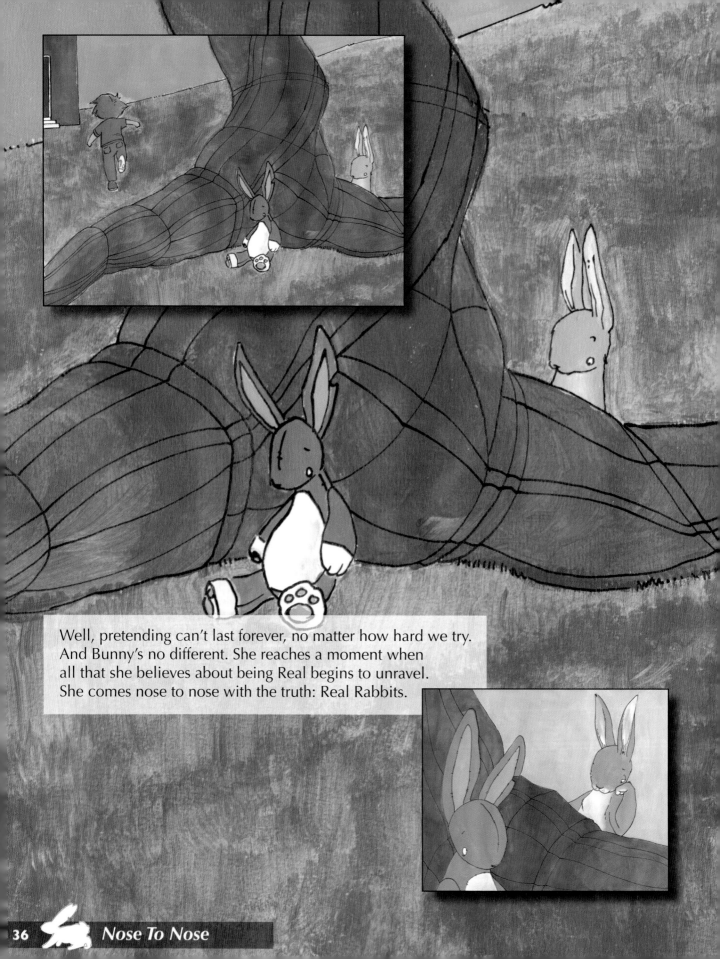

Well, pretending can't last forever, no matter how hard we try. And Bunny's no different. She reaches a moment when all that she believes about being Real begins to unravel. She comes nose to nose with the truth: Real Rabbits.

Nose To Nose

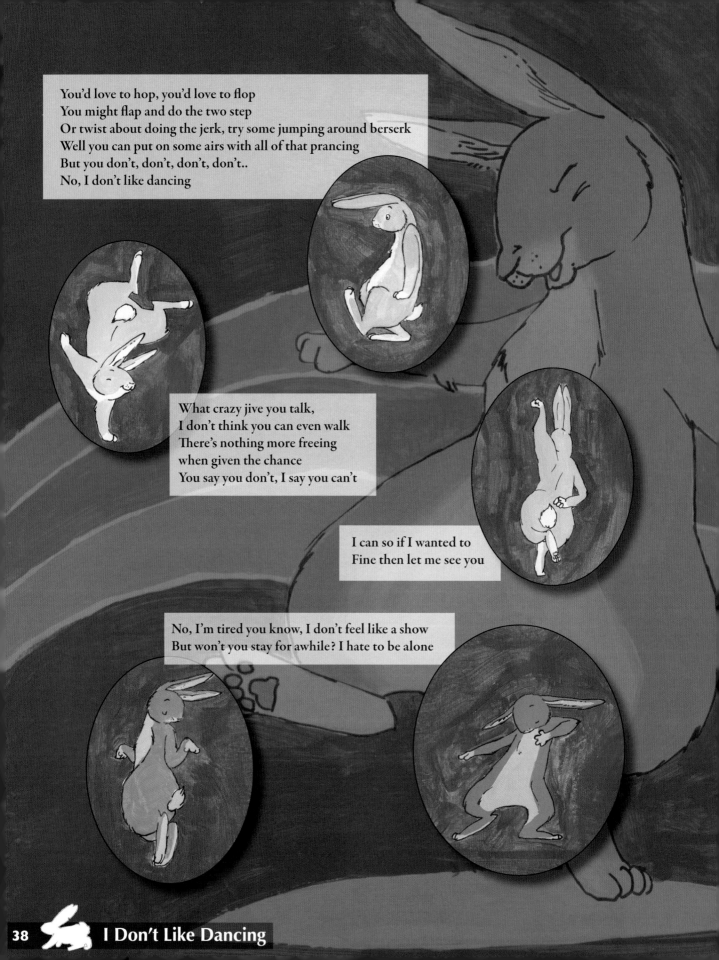

You'd love to hop, you'd love to flop
You might flap and do the two step
Or twist about doing the jerk, try some jumping around berserk
Well you can put on some airs with all of that prancing
But you don't, don't, don't, don't..
No, I don't like dancing

What crazy jive you talk,
I don't think you can even walk
There's nothing more freeing
when given the chance
You say you don't, I say you can't

I can so if I wanted to
Fine then let me see you

No, I'm tired you know, I don't feel like a show
But won't you stay for awhile? I hate to be alone

Nah, you don't like dancing
I've never given it thought
Right, you don't like dancing
Maybe I've never been taught

There'll be no hop and no flop
You won't flap and do the two step
Or twist about doing the jerk,
and there's no jumping around berserk
You won't put on no airs with all of that prancing

But you don't, don't, don't, don't..
No, I don't like dancing

Just let me sniff you
And then I'll know if you
Are really alive or really a lie
Crawling up next to you
I can smell right through you
Your scent is sawdust and that you can't deny

I can't believe this Bunny's deal
It isn't even real

I am too, I am true
I'm real just ask the Boy. . .

Just ask the Boy, ask the Boy
Just ask the Boy Just ask the Boy...
Just ask the Boy, ask the Boy

Real to a little boy is one thing; but Real to Real Rabbits is quite another.
Bunny stubbornly holds onto the only "truth" she has.
To the Real Rabbits, she screams she's Real. "Just ask the Boy; just ask the Boy."
What the Boy would have said, we don't know. For what we do know
is that little Boys have Real germs and they get Real sick.

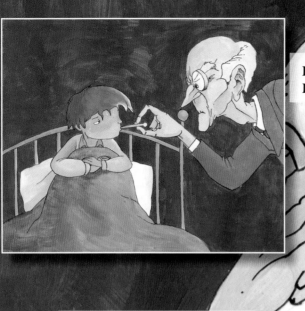

I've detected the symptoms, the runny nose and cough
I'll prescribe medications and we'll chase this cold off

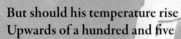

But should his temperature rise
Upwards of a hundred and five

Then it's Scarlet Fever, Scarlet Fever
And I regret to say good God's being bad today
If he takes a little life away
With Scarlet Fever, Scarlet Fever
I dare not deceive, my medicine may fail to relieve
If another little life slips away

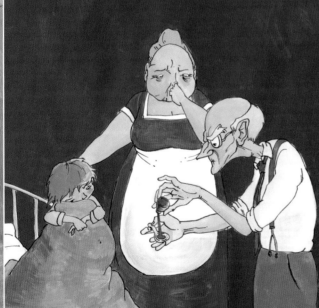

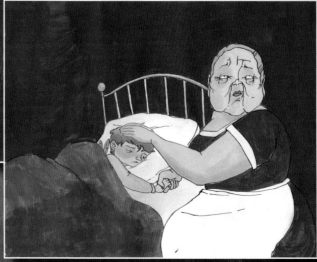

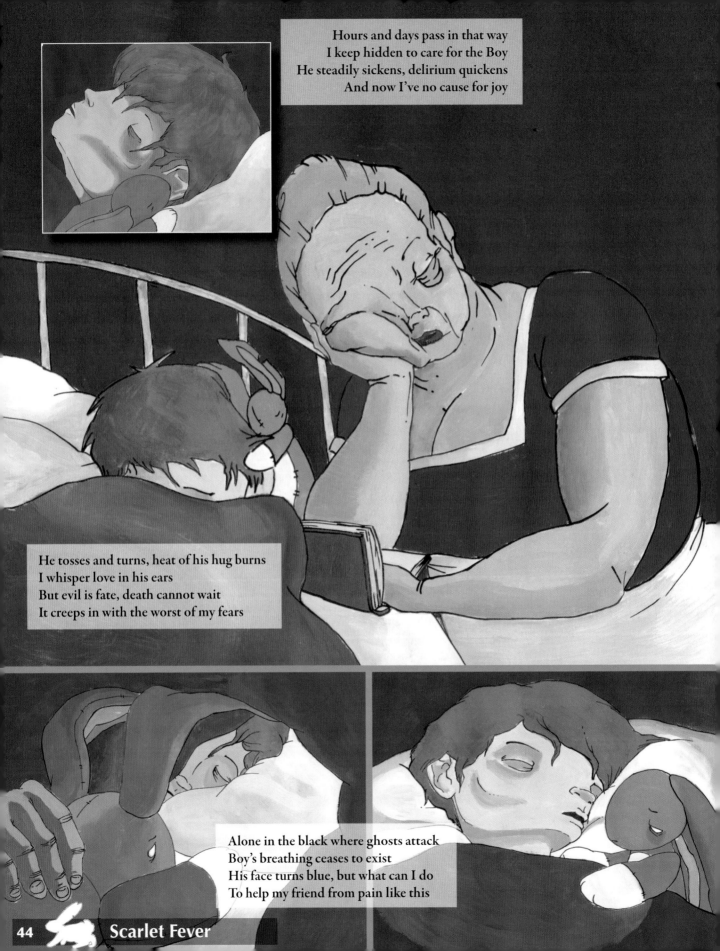

Hours and days pass in that way
I keep hidden to care for the Boy
He steadily sickens, delirium quickens
And now I've no cause for joy

He tosses and turns, heat of his hug burns
I whisper love in his ears
But evil is fate, death cannot wait
It creeps in with the worst of my fears

Alone in the black where ghosts attack
Boy's breathing ceases to exist
His face turns blue, but what can I do
To help my friend from pain like this

I'm scared and it's cold, life's leaving his hold
I wish I could save him for good
What point is living if it ends unforgiving
I wish I could save him I would,
If I could save him I would
If I could save him I would

It's Scarlet Fever, Scarlet Fever
I know that you need me, hold on and don't leave me
Let me give my little life away
Scarlet Fever, Scarlet Fever
Please let the Boy live to laugh and play
I don't want to be real if real is this way
I'd give my little life, I'd give my little life
I'd give my little life away

Boy opens his eyes, his chest starts to rise
And hugging me just like he did before he says,
I love you Bunny
My, my, life is funny
But I can't remember anymore...
Remember...

Remember, remember, remember...

We alone are the real in this place...

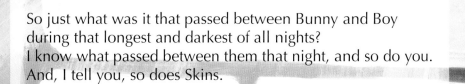

So just what was it that passed between Bunny and Boy
during that longest and darkest of all nights?
I know what passed between them that night, and so do you.
And, I tell you, so does Skins.

Humble us, humor us
Humor us, humble us please

Now there's so little time

If you humble us, humor us
Humor us, humble us please

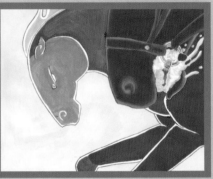

And that's all we'll desire

Oh let it all be way beyond our grasp
And it shall be or maybe not perhaps

If you humble us, humor us
Humor us, humble us please

Now there's so little time

If you Humble us, humor us
Humor us, humble us please

And that's all we'll desire
Oh please, that's all we'll desire

Oh let it all be as it's meant to be
And it shall be ordained as destiny

If you humble us, humor us
Humor us, humble us please

Now there's so little time

If you humble us, humor us
Humor us, humble us please

And that's all we'll desire
Ooh, yeah that's all we'll desire

Oh let it all be way beyond our grasp
And it shall be or maybe not perhaps

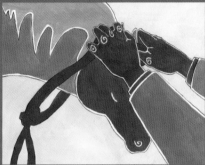
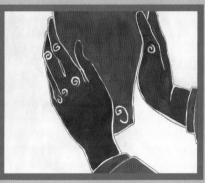

When you humble us, humor us
Humor us, humble us please

Now there's so little time

If you humble us, humor us
Humor us, humble us please
And that's all we'll desire

Yeah there's so little time
And you're all, all we'll desire
Oh Lord, Oh Lord now
We are relying on your love
Even now, we are relying on your love...

Oh Doctor, Doctor the Boy is awake
Of course I knew his fever would break
It's a miracle, thank God he's saved
It's simple science, for heaven's sake

Oh Doctor, Doctor what do you guess
We should do with all of this mess?
His Bunny and the dirty bed-dress
Poor child he seems so restless

The Germs, Germs, Germs, They're so cantankerous
The Germs, Germs, Germs, They're awfully dangerous
The Germs, Germs, Germs, Are awfully dangerous
The Germs, Germs, Germs,
Keep the Germs away from us
Keep the Germs away from us

Doctor, Doctor, am I well once again?
May I play in the woods and sand?
Go seek and find what's in store
Mind your health, your coat's by the door

Doctor, Doctor, what about his Bunny?
That old thing couldn't have cost much money
Shall I throw it out with the contaminate?
Better burn it all and never hesitate

The Germs, Germs, Germs, They're awfully dangerous
The Germs, Germs, Germs, They're so cantankerous
The Germs, Germs, Germs, Are awfully dangerous
The Germs, Germs, Germs,
Keep the Germs away from us
Keep the Germs away from us

Tonight the gardener will blaze us a fire
I'll leave this bag to burn out back for the pyre
And I sing so long, so long, so long,
So long, so long, so long,
So long, so long, so long,
So long Bunny
So long...

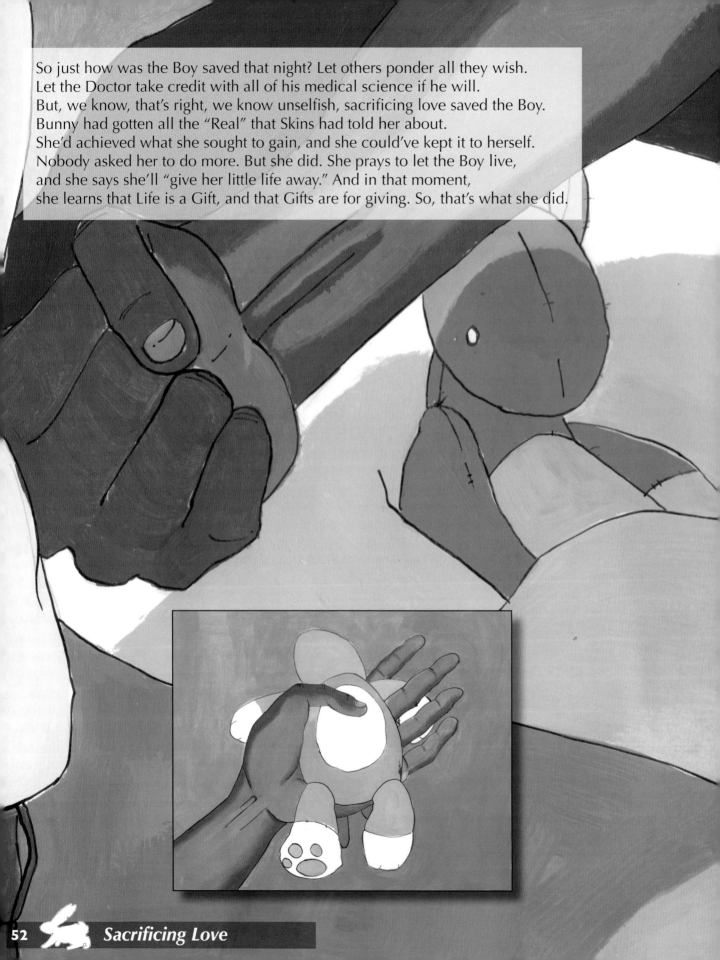

So just how was the Boy saved that night? Let others ponder all they wish.
Let the Doctor take credit with all of his medical science if he will.
But, we know, that's right, we know unselfish, sacrificing love saved the Boy.
Bunny had gotten all the "Real" that Skins had told her about.
She'd achieved what she sought to gain, and she could've kept it to herself.
Nobody asked her to do more. But she did. She prays to let the Boy live,
and she says she'll "give her little life away." And in that moment,
she learns that Life is a Gift, and that Gifts are for giving. So, that's what she did.

And in return for that unselfish act, she waits to be burned in the fire. Or does she?
Now friends, I told you I've been around for awhile,
I've done lots of things. I've seen some things you'd be amazed at.
But for now, let's just say, I'm the Gardener, and this is where I come in.

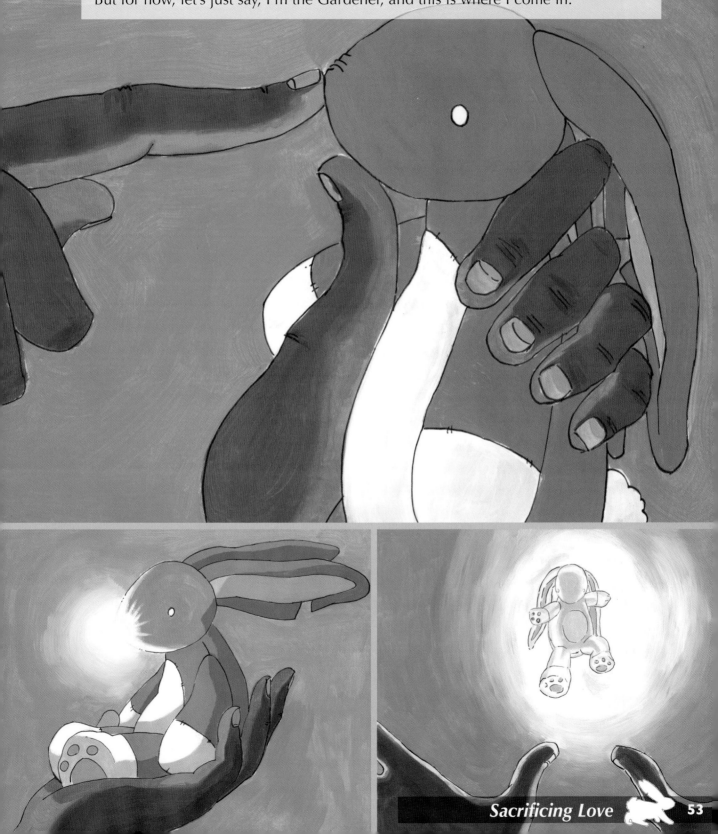

In every life there comes a choice
Just as thoughts give way to voice
For what you say and do, you choose
Yeah you are all that's defining you

You were mild, you were meek
That's what the righteous seek, now so to speak
You'll get to live free
Baby believe me
You were good, so good, you gave, you gave, you gave your life away
So now for real, for real, for real for real you shall stay
For real for real...

For Real For Real

I thought that I was already real
Only to the Boy as a toy that was the deal
I prayed that he would be alright
That's how you learned of love's sacrifice

You were mild, you were meek
That's what the righteous seek, now so to speak
You'll get to live free
Baby believe me
You were good, so good, you gave, you gave, you gave your life away
So now for real, for real, for real for real you shall stay
For real for real... Ooh, Ooh, Ooh...

You were mild, you were meek
That's what the righteous seek, now so to speak
You'll get to live free
Baby believe me
You were good, so good, you gave, you gave, you gave your life away
So now for real, for real, for real for real you shall stay
For real for real...

For Real For Real

You were mild, you were meek
That's what the righteous seek, now so to speak
You'll get to live free
Baby believe me
You were good, so good, you gave, you gave, you gave your life away

So now for real, for real you shall stay
For real for real

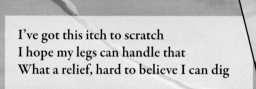

I've got this itch to scratch
I hope my legs can handle that
What a relief, hard to believe I can dig

At last I know where I belong
I've found some friends who love my song
Forevermore, I'm on all fours, can't you dig?

Who don't love dancing?
A whimsical waltz to a French foxtrot
Who don't love dancing?
A moonlit march hoedown hits the spot

And you can hop, you can flop
Try the flap, it's a two step
Or strut about doing the jerk
Doing the robot, if you can make it work

This ain't putting on airs
It's a rhythmic romancing
And no I don't know no, know nobody who
Who don't love dancing?

Go twist out your blues friend
The mash potato can't lose friend
So who don't love dancing?

Who Don't Love Dancing?

Every living thing, growing or grown
Grab yourself a partner or just cut it alone
Say don't you love dancing?

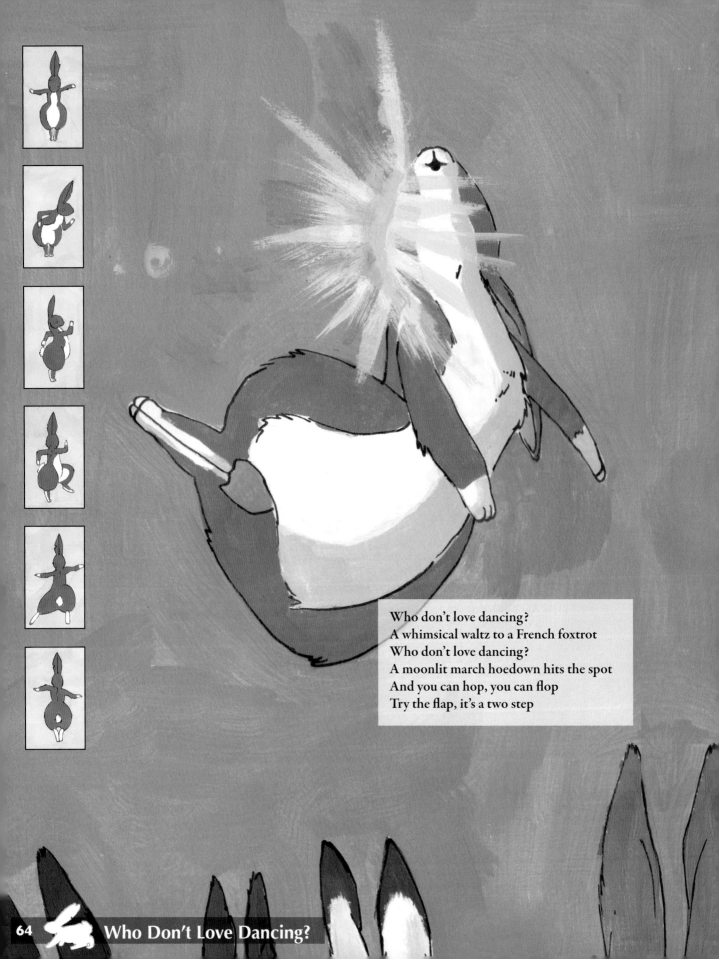

Who don't love dancing?
A whimsical waltz to a French foxtrot
Who don't love dancing?
A moonlit march hoedown hits the spot
And you can hop, you can flop
Try the flap, it's a two step

Or strut about doing the jerk
Doing the robot, if you can make it work
This ain't putting on airs
It's a rhythmic romancing
And no I don't know no, know nobody who
Who don't love dancing?

Who don't love dancing? Who don't love dancing?

Well, friends, that's something to think about.
You don't become really Real just by being loved,
And you don't have Life by holding on to the one you have.
Only when you give it away for love will you truly live.
After all, Life's a Gift. What will you do with yours?

Truly Live

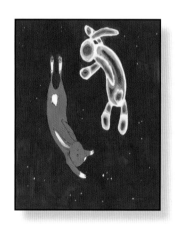

fin

The Velveteen Rabbit
An Illustrated Rock Opera

performed by
Ruin Statue

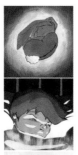
Wendi Freeman as Bunny, The Velveteen Rabbit

Ricky Dymes as The Boy

Monte "Jass" Wells as Skins, An Old & Weathered Toy Horse

Gigi Georgie as Nana, The Boy's Guardian

Crane Nutthousen as Doctor, MD

Jack Potts as Gibb Gray, The Real Rabbit

Virgil Jenkins, Sr. as Timothy, The Wooden Lion

Sir Richard Alnamax as The Thinker-Bot

Larry Dinglewood as The Strongman-Bot

Swayne MacVicious as HMS, The Model Sailboat

and
Arnell Pleasant
as Art, The Narrator

featuring
Background Vocals by
The Hall Portraits